Bilingual Edition

LET'S LOOK AT FEELINGS™

Edición Bilingüe

What I Look Like When I Am Angry

Cómo me veo cuando estoy enojado

Heidi Johansen
Traducción al español:
María Cristina Brusca

The Rosen Publishing Group's
PowerStart Press™ & **Editorial Buenas Letras**™
New York

1

For Mamacita

Published in 2004 by The Rosen Publishing Group, Inc.
29 East 21st Street, New York, NY 10010

First Edition

Book Design: Kim Sonsky
Photo Credits: All photos by Maura B. McConnell.

Library of Congress Cataloging-in-Publication Data

Johansen, Heidi Leigh.
[What I look like when I am angry. Spanish & English]
What I look like when I am angry = Como me veo cuando estoy enojado / Heidi Leigh Johansen ; translated by María Cristina Brusca.
    p. cm. — (Let's look at feelings)
Summary: Describes what different parts of the face look like when a person is angry. Spanish and English.
Includes index.
  ISBN 1-4042-7508-8 (library binding)
1. Anger in children—Juvenile literature. [1. Anger. 2. Facial expression. 3. Emotions. 4. Spanish language material—Bilingual.]
I. Title: Como me veo cuando estoy enojado. II. Title. III. Series.
  BF723.A4J6318 2004
  152.4'7— dc21

2003009107

Manufactured in the United States of America

Due to the changing nature of Internet links, PowerKids Press has developed an online list of Web sites related to the subject of this book. This site is updated regularly. Please use this link to access the list:

http://www.buenasletraslinks.com/llafe/enojado/

Contents

Contenido

I am angry.

_____

Estoy enojada.

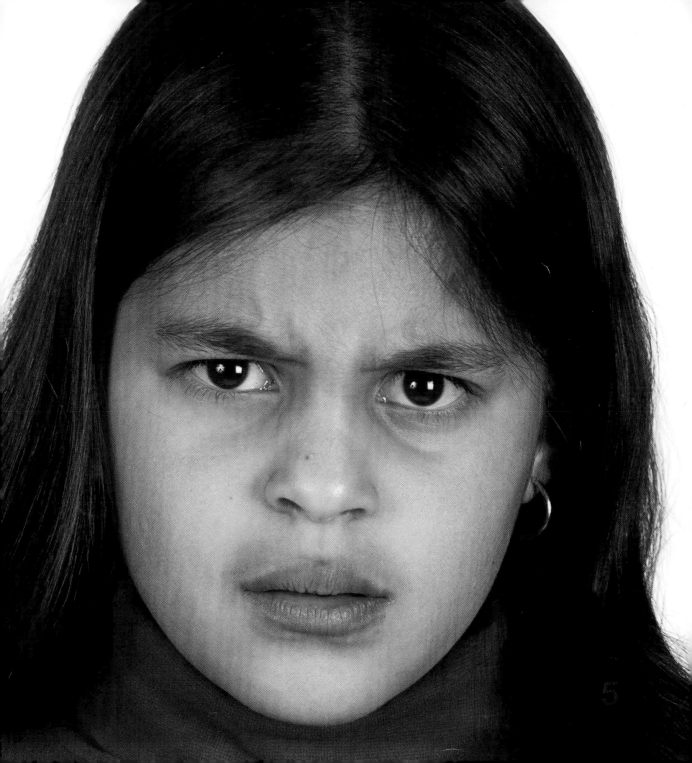

5

When I am angry my eyebrows go down.

Cuando estoy enojada, mis cejas se fruncen.

My eyes are small when I am angry.

Mis ojos se ven pequeños, cuando estoy enojado.

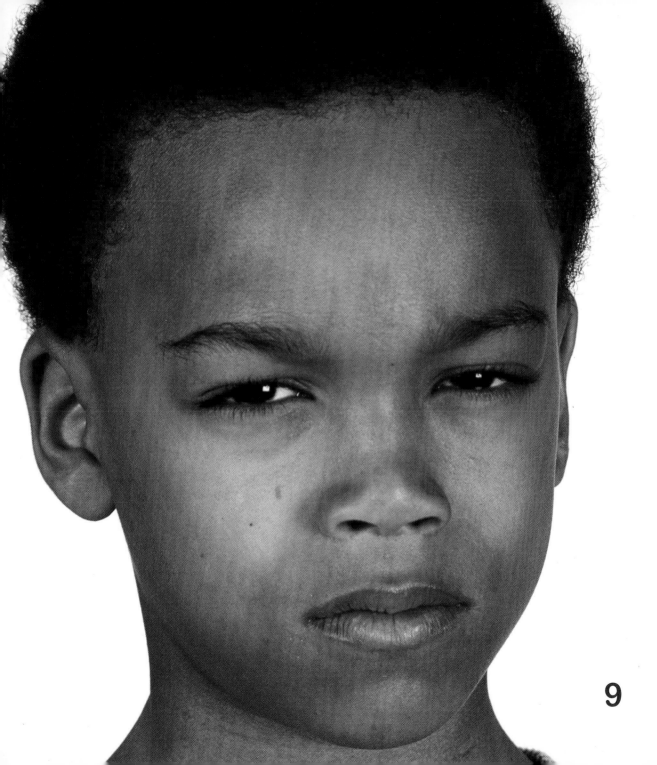

9

There are lines on my nose when I am angry.

Se forman líneas en mi nariz, cuando estoy enojado.

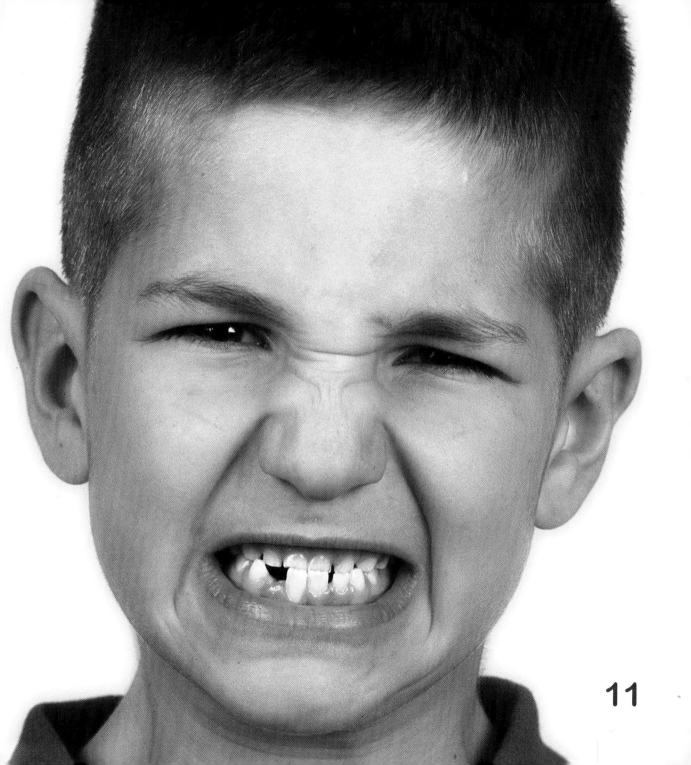

11

Both sides of my mouth go down when I am angry.

Los dos lados de mi boca se tuercen hacia abajo, cuando estoy enojado.

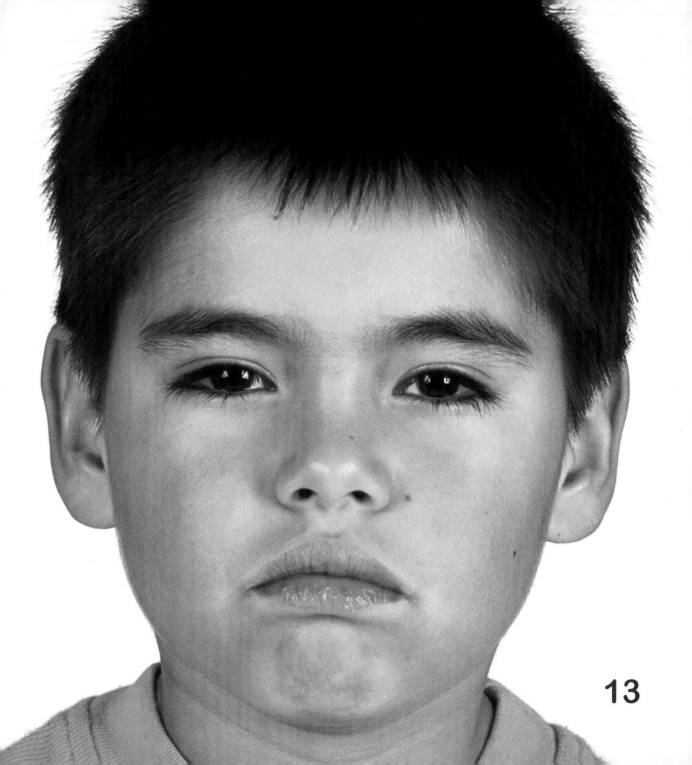

13

My mouth is closed tight
when I am angry.

Mi boca se cierra,
muy apretada, cuando
estoy enojada.

You can see my teeth when
I am angry.

_____

Puedes ver mis dientes,
cuando estoy enojada.

My mouth opens in a yell when I am angry.

Mi boca se abre en un grito, cuando estoy enojada.

When I am angry my face is red.

Cuando estoy enojado, mi cara se pone roja.

21

This is what I look like when I am angry.

Así me veo cuando estoy enojada.

23

Words to Know
Palabras que debes saber

eyebrow
ceja

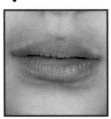

mouth
boca

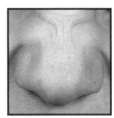

nose
nariz

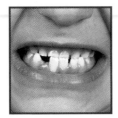

teeth
dientes

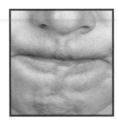

tight
apretado

Index

Índice